THIRTY YEARS OF BASEBALL THROUGH THE LENS OF WALTER IOOSS

DIAMOND DREAMS

INTRODUCTION BY WALTER IOOSS

TEXT BY TOM BOSWELL

LITTLE, BROWN AND COMPANY

BOSTON NEW YORK TORONTO LONDON

First Edition

ISBN 0-316-42012-3

Library of Congress Catalog Card Number 95-77073

10 9 8 7 6 5 4 3 2 1

NIL

Published simultaneously in Canada by Little, Brown & Company (Canada) Limited

Printed in Italy

Produced by:

Rare Air, Ltd.
A Mark Vancil Company
130 Washington
West Dundee, IL 60118

Designed by:

John Vieceli
McMillan Associates
130 Washington
West Dundee, IL 60118

Special Thanks to:

Michael McMillan, Anne McMillan, Laura Vancil and Paul Sheridan.

END LEAVES: CONNIE MACK STADIUM, 1965

PAGE 1: KEVIN MITCHELL, 1993, CANDLESTICK PARK

<< RAFAEL SANTANA, 1986, SHEA STADIUM

TED WILLIAMS, 1960, YANKEE STADIUM >

WRIGLEY FIELD, 1985 >>

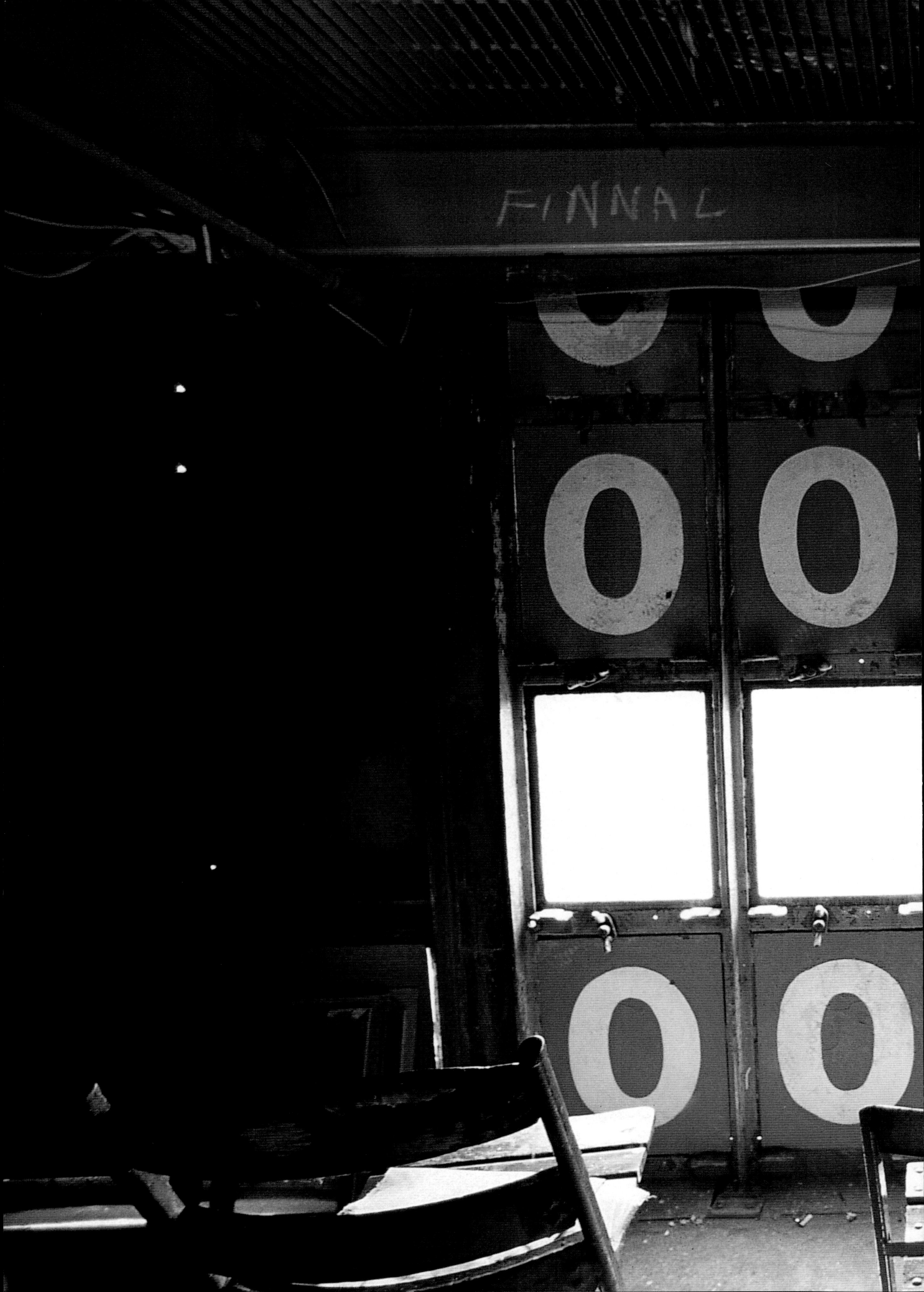
FINNAL

INTRODUCTION

BY WALTER IOOSS

If there is a single thread that has connected the various stages of my life, as well as my photographic career, it has been baseball. As a child, the game and its beauty provided a unique common ground for me and my father. Baseball and photography were his passions. In the early 1960s, they became mine as well.

For a photographer, memories of individual shots are as poignant as those of the players themselves. Every shot has a story, and as I selected the photographs for this book, I recalled many of them.

Like the shot of Tom Seaver (pages 14-15) which was taken at Tampa's Lopez Field in 1969. I was captivated by this background. And I am still intrigued by Seaver. He always remembered my name and seemed interested in my life. Highly unusual for a player.

The portrait of Michael Jordan (page 24) was taken early one morning in Sarasota. Michael is always punctual. But this day he had arrived a little later than the scheduled 7:15 a.m. My assistant was in the dugout about 500 feet away. Michael says, "We have to shoot here and now." All I had was one camera and 20-35 mm zoom. Michael says, "Walter, don't show my legs." I said, "Don't worry, you can trust me."

As with Michael, anyone who met Casey Stengel adored him. Unlike Michael, Casey never remembered my name or, as it turns out, anyone else's. As a 20-year-old photographer always hanging around the team, I couldn't understand why he never knew who I was. The shot on page 115 was taken in St. Petersburg in 1964. I later realized Casey couldn't remember any of our names, including Mickey Mantle's when he came up from the minors. He called

everyone "Kid." On my first spring training assignment for *Sports Illustrated*, I checked into the Colonial Inn, which is where the Mets were staying. What struck me was the banner hanging at the hotel. I had been the studio photographer at Chess Records so I was used to seeing groups with one star like Martha and the Vandellas. The banner in Tampa read, "Welcome Casey Stengel and the N.Y. Mets."

Baseball's pregame routine is virtually the same with every team every year. And it starts with batting practice. I caught Walt Hriniak (page 42) throwing batting practice at Fenway Park in 1979. The white dots are silver seat numbers reflecting the late afternoon light that were blown out of focus by a 600 mm lens.

Players have an amazing ability to remember minute details about specific games and ballparks. I gave Roger

Clemens a print of the shot on page 55 and asked him if he remembered where it was taken. He took one look and said, "Road uniform, double mound, grey-brown dirt. Baltimore."

Photographers sometimes have the same kind of memory on certain shots. For some reason, I still remember what happened when Roberto Clemente (page 58) threw his bat at that outside pitch. I had never seen anything like it before. He lined a double down the right-field line.

But it was the freedom we had in those days that made the game so fascinating. There were virtually no restrictions on where photographers could move around the field. That's what made the shots of Frank Robinson (pages 78-79) possible. These were taken in Baltimore in 1966. My favorite baseball photograph came from that same era. The shot of Connie Mack Stadium

(page 43) was taken in 1966. In the years since, I've realized it's the only original I have from that night. I have no idea where the others went.

Even when I stopped shooting sporting events exclusively in 1984, I continued to make my way back to the ballparks at least twice a season. The *Iooss Baseball Card Collection* I shot for The Upper Deck Company in 1992 helped bring this book up to date. But it was a similar shoot for Upper Deck in 1993 that made this project a reality. I was allowed to do what I had always enjoyed the most. That is, 'Shoot whatever you think looks good.'

However, I do want to apologize to players that deserved a place in this book but were not included. The reason is simple: The quality of the photographs didn't warrant the space.

I would like to thank all the people around the game, most notably the

players, for trusting me and taking the time to pose over the years; *Sports Illustrated*, an institution that has been such an enormous factor in my life since 1961; The Upper Deck Company and V. J. Lovero, who brought me back into the game; my father, Walter Iooss, who passed his passion for the game and artistic eyes on to me; and my wife, Eva, and sons, Christian and Bjorn, for enduring my absences; and finally, my mother, who has always been my greatest fan.

As I worked on this project, I continued to think back to the time when everything in my life seemed to revolve around baseball. From stickball on the streets of Brooklyn to the A. P. B. A. baseball games, and that wonderful feeling you got as a kid putting on your baseball uniform. I hope *Diamond Dreams* allows others to capture, even for a moment, those same kinds of feelings.

SCORECARD

SPRING TRAINING IS THE BEST. Don't let anybody tell you different. It's got tons of what's best in baseball with only ounces of what's worst. Actually, Sarasota in February or Tempe in March has plenty of what's best in life. Overlooking spring training is like forgetting to visit the Grand Canyon. ⚾ No matter how often you remind yourself to dress lightly and in layers, you're still never prepared for Florida or Arizona in what's supposed to be winter. It's not just the heat. Thank God, it's the humidity, too. The damp air hugs you like a lei. "Shorts!" you think. "How fast can I get into shorts, a T-shirt and no socks?" ⚾ Spring training is all about stripping down. Baseball, when the scores don't

SPRING

count, reminds us of how little it takes to be truly happy. We need sunshine, warmth and a breeze, of course. The smell of fresh grass and dust mixed with the aroma of pretzels and beer certainly helps. Got allergies? Get 'em revved up. For perfection, we'd request a glint of big water in the distance and perhaps the sight of seagulls above our outfielders. ⚾ Let's pare to the core. Put your feet on the back of the seat in front of you, then lay the nape of your neck on the cool railing behind. Smell, taste, see, touch and feel as though for the first time or last. ⚾ Big fancy ballparks? Don't need 'em. Less grandstand means more sky. Let the clouds, the weather and the sunset into the park without obstruction. Five thousand seats, not 50,000, means we sit 10 times closer. Who knew billboards were so vivid? ⚾ We need

Ed Kranepool, 1969, St. Petersburg

<< Tom Seaver, 1981, Tampa

342

we're the

PYRAMID SCH

6510 N. 5

DIVISION OF

companions and activity, a sense that we're still part of the world. Yet we want escape, too. No telephones can ring. Beepers get booed. We want economy—of motion, of emotion. A clean motel, mornings at the beach, then hot dogs and a bleacher ticket in the afternoon. Where else could a life so cheap feel like paradise for so long? ⚾ You could put up a sign on every grapefruit league wall that said, "No idiots allowed." But you don't need them, do you? No idiots come. Spring training is a self-governing paradise. Only your friends want to be there. Including, of course, the friends you just haven't met yet. ⚾ "We'd give an autograph to anybody who was here today," Jim Palmer once said. "But then, the people who are here today aren't the kind who would ask for an autograph. They're my idea of good baseball fans. Anybody who comes to watch you run wind sprints and play catch and cover first base on bunts obviously has a feeling for the game. They're always good people to talk to." ⚾ Your true grassroots jackasses just naturally feel out of place in spring training. You'll never see Howard Stern or Rush Limbaugh. Not important enough for them. Nor, perhaps, would they be important enough at it. ⚾ Spring training is personal, intimate, never lived in capital letters. It's the game's six-week-long reunion with the batting cage as watering hole. ⚾ Spring training seduces you when you're young and can't get your heart to slow down. In middle age, it holds you tight when that same heart gets heavy 'cause your life won't slow down. And it still embraces you when you're old with a heart that could stop any minute. It's a thrill or an elixir or a final meditation without depression. Whatever you need. Who loves ya, baby?

HA

C A R L T O N

Once, Steve Carlton appeared before me in the Phillies dugout with a bat on his shoulder. "You have no right to look at my locker. I heard you looked at my locker," he said, repeating several times. "You've made a big mistake."

From that moment, perhaps I should have known that Carlton would end up living in a half-built underground bunker on an isolated ranch in the West, believing in international conspiracies involving everyone from a group of Jewish bankers to a Roman round table of 300 that controls the world. Instead, I just thought, "No wonder he doesn't talk. He doesn't want everybody to know that he sounds half-cracked."

As you study Carlton's attire in his portrait, let the Alfred Hitchcock background music play in your head.

Only one hitter completely owned Carlton—Johnny Bench, who said, "It's like I'm thinking along with him." Once, when hunting with teammate Joe Hoerner, Carlton missed a bird, then fired off a shot into the air. "There," said Carlton, apropos of nothing. "That one's for Bench."

At his peak, Carlton wore earplugs when he pitched, demanded that he have his own personal catcher (Tim McCarver) and meditated for an hour before each start. He preferred Eastern philosophies or est, though he'd try anything, so long as it fed into his Ubermensch superiority complex. In the Phils media guide, Carlton once listed his favorite musicians as Jascha Heifetz and Jean-Pierre Rampal, then added that the people he'd most like to meet were Socrates, Einstein, Thomas Jefferson, Napoleon, Jesus Christ and Gandhi.

"The batter hardly exists for Steve," said McCarver. "He's playing an elevated game of catch."

Carlton ended his career with a 329-244 record, a 3.22 ERA and 56 shutouts in 5,217 innings. Ironically, the contemporary pitcher most completely opposite to Carlton—the normal, funny, self-deprecating, unimposing Don Sutton—has a 324-256 record with a 3.26 ERA and 58 shutouts in 5,282 innings. Both pitched in five League Championship Series and four World Series with a 6-4 record. Both retired after 1988. Yet Carlton, because of his mystique and strikeouts, got into the Hall of Fame on the first ballot. Sutton is, at this writing, still waiting.

Who says it helps to be nice to the press?

< STEVE CARLTON, 1973, CLEARWATER

SAM McDOWELL, 1974, BRADENTON >>

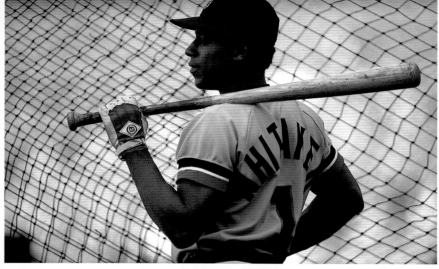

Walt Alston, 1982, Holman Stadium

Y O G I

In his playing days, Yogi Berra was infamous for mooching personal products from his teammates. If you left a comb or toothpaste or razor in your locker, Yogi would treat it as community property. Whitey Ford, who lockered next to Yogi, decided to get revenge for this annoying petty thievery by his batterymate.

Ford was a master do-it-yourself guy. He'd make various rasps and patches of sandpaper for his glove and uniform to help him add scuffball magic to his repertoire. This time, Whitey turned his ingenuity to a tube of roll-on deodorant. Somehow, he filled the thing with glue. Ford know his stinky catcher couldn't resist. Yogi took the bait. The locker room waited. Soon enough, Yogi was howling. As the Yankees laughed until they cried, the team trainer had to shave Yogi's arm away from his sides.

Does it still sting just a little?

YES, THIS IS SUMMER—a day so perfect that it seems to glory in being a cliché. Wrigley Field. Afternoon game. Blue sky. Huge, indolent cumulus clouds watching over the Cubs. Will they blow the lead in the eighth or ninth? ⚾ This, also, is summer. The magenta afterglow behind the left-field pavilion in Dodger Stadium. If you walk up a few rows from field level, you'll begin to see the San Gabriel Mountains beyond the ballpark, like some ludicrously improbable Hollywood back-lot mural. Nothing should be this beautiful, you think. Then you understand why the Dodgers sold out every game for decades. ⚾ And this is summer, too. A night game in St. Louis with a child leaning on your shoulder, asking questions and

SUMMER

wheedling for another ice cream bar. The father in Walter's shot is a genius. He's gotten a seat in the back row so the boy can *roam*. Anyone who's lived this picture knows the hell-on-earth of keeping a six-year-old in one seat in the middle of a row for three hours. ⚾ The core of baseball is the 100-or-so games a season which are played on days and nights like these when the hype of Opening Day is long past and the promise of the pennant race and the World Series is barely on the horizon. If you love the game, these are the scenes of which you never tire, even though, with the years, it seems reasonable that you should. As Earl Weaver said, "This ain't a football game. We do this every day." ⚾ Summer baseball casts a different spell. One warm night in Camden Yards, I couldn't get myself to leave the ballpark and go home, despite a three-hour rain delay.

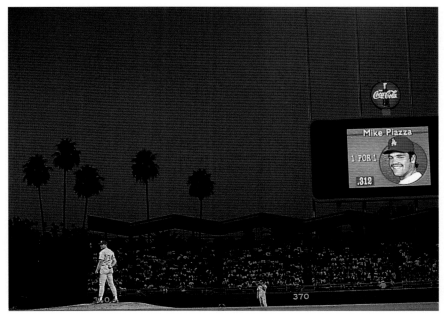

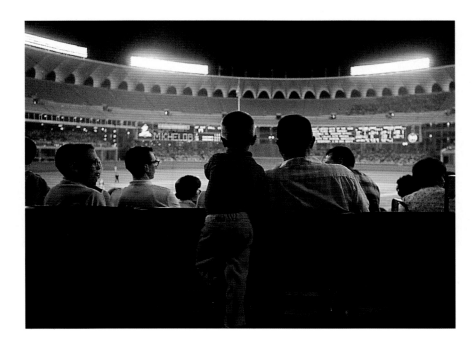

^
WRIGLEY FIELD, 1985; DODGER STADIUM, 1993; BUSCH STADIUM, 1968

WILLIE STARGELL, 1977, THREE RIVERS STADIUM

FENWAY PARK, 1992 >>

Midnight passed, a breeze awoke itself. The emptier the stadium became, the more beautiful it seemed. Eventually, 5,000 of us were left—everybody sitting in the seat he'd always coveted but probably couldn't get. The park, with 40,000 empty seats stacked above us, felt like a deep green cavern with lights. The whole scene looked like every Washington Senators home game of the 1960s—a private party, a private joke, for an extremely odd but gentle group of people. ● Finally, the drizzle stopped. Several Orioles gathered in front of us to do their stretching. Their white uniforms—many probably freshly donned during the long delay—were spotless. Cal Ripken—the stoic Prisoner of the Streak who seldom changes expression on the field—jogged up behind them. He planned his attack perfectly. With one giant leap-frog hop into the largest puddle, he drenched every dry pair of pants in the bunch. Maybe Cal hadn't laughed that hard in public in years. ● Summer nights are the source of almost all baseball lore with any tang. Nobody lets their hair down at those post-season media circuses with 2,000 reporters on hand. But, at Game No. 97, with a few beat reporters idly stirring the pot, anybody might say anything. "I'm not going to second-guess Dallas Green," you might hear Whitey Herzog drawl. "All I'm going to say is that he just traded his best pitcher for a sack of shit." ● Baseball in the summer is scenes and quips and sundowns and a fan tying a string around the neck of a rubber chicken, then dropping it over the dugout roof so that, with luck, Willie Stargell will sign it. Sometimes you wonder which came first, the chicken or the sport. Is baseball just an excuse in this frazzled world to sit in one lovely spot for a few warm hours and, between sunsets and conversations, get your rubber chicken autographed?

H R I N I A K

Baseball is a game with rituals inside rituals. Over the interminable months and years, as you move from town to town, it's necessary for the sake of sanity to put some spin on each and every habitual act.

For instance, look at the basket of balls next to Walt Hriniak in this picture during batting practice. A photographer sees the sun glinting off the right-field bleachers in Fenway Park, mimicking the visual effect of the balls in the coach's sack. A baseball beat writer might see that bag differently.

A handful of times a season, you'll see some old coach or one of the team's scrubs racing around the infield like a madman during BP, picking up all the stray balls and tossing them in this bag. He'll be moving much too fast, causing too much of a fuss, perhaps even yelling or feigning anger. Anything to catch the eye of the few thousand early-arriving fans in the stands.

Then, his arms hugging the full-to-the-brim ball bag, he'll run to the top of the pitching mound, pretend to trip over the rubber and, with a horrifying scream, spin in a circle as if he'd been shot by a machine gun. If the pratfall is executed perfectly, 100 balls will fly out of the bag in all directions just as the coach-comedian collapses on his face in the grass.

The team then grades the coach on 1) crowd reaction, 2) ball dispersion and 3) degree-of-difficulty-and-risk of the phony "accident."

Ray Miller, pitching coach of the Pittsburgh Pirates, could stagger, stumble, pretend to catch his balance, then go tumbling two or three more times before he actually collapsed, as if dead, just as the last ball left his bag. He once got an ovation from the Yankee Stadium crowd.

"I only do it a couple of times a season," Miller said. "You don't want it to get old hat. Sooner or later, I'm going to cripple myself."

^

Connie Mack Stadium, 1966

< *Walt Hriniak, 1979, Fenway Park*

Reggie Sanders, 1993, Dodger Stadium >>

Dwight Gooden, 1985, St. Petersburg

DWIGHT GOODEN, 1985, ST. PETERSBURG

One sweltering afternoon in Wrigley Field, bullpen coach
Johnny Oates went to the locker room for a catcher's mitt in the
sixth inning. Oates was glad to escape the 100-degree pen for
the air-conditioned clubhouse. Once there, Oates discovered the
Cubs' star reliever Lee Smith, lying on the cool concrete floor.

"He was fast asleep," said Oates, "his chest covered with

quickly. With age, he added pitches to his repertoi
from a prototypic power pitcher to a corner-nippi
artist. Teammates appreciated his fatherly, teasing
Pitching coaches respected his intelligence, experi
calm in crisis.

However, baseball could never forgive Lee's si

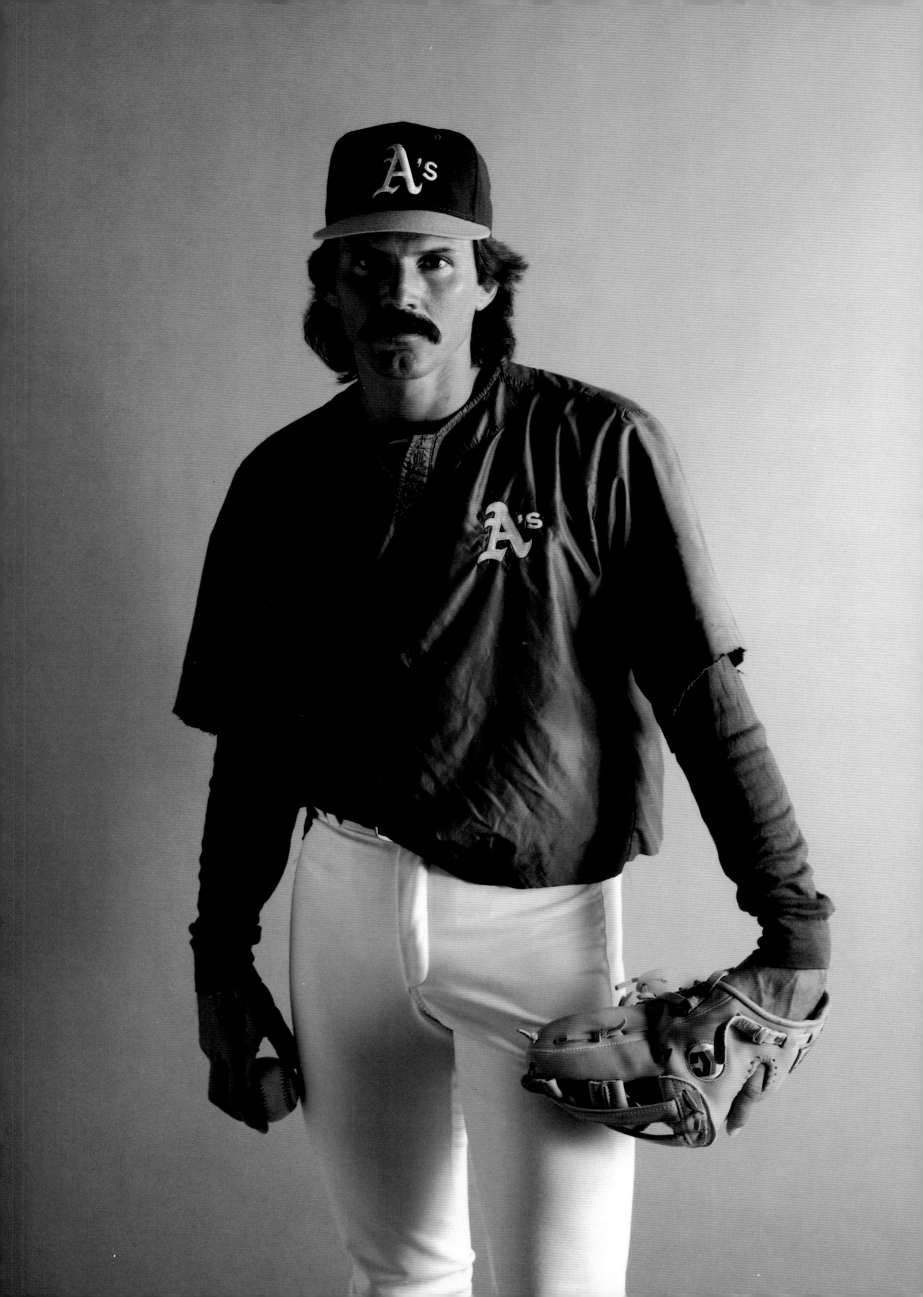

J O H N

Tommy John, the 288-game winner, was known for his religiosity, charitable works, occasional stutter and aging choirboy smile. Also, he looked as clumsy as your uncle Fred. He lunged. He short-armed the ball like a man throwing a large, heavy dart. Some days, half his pitches seemed to reach the catcher on one short skip. The hidden component in John was his ferocious competitiveness.

"I have four basic pitches—fastball, curve, slider and change-up—plus eight illegal ones," John, said with an enigmatic smile. By the end of his career, hitters said they weren't sure he really had the four legal ones.

Once, I asked John why hitters could never seem to guess what he'd throw. "Because," said John, "I always subtract one ball from the actual count. I'm pitching with a different scoreboard than they are." What happens when the count is 3-0 with the bases loaded? Surely, he must give in then. "No," said John. "There's still a base open. Home plate."

∧
Tommy John, 1979, Metropolitan Stadium

≪ Tim Pugh, 1993, Dodger Stadium

Nolan Ryan pitched his seventh career no-hitter at the age of 44. Throughout the game's locker room and clubhouses, news of the deed brought stunned, disbelieving silence. In Baltimore, one veteran—Randy Milligan—found words to describe how Ryan had gradually grown fantastical and legendary, even as he played in their midst. Fortunately, Milligan said it in jock-speak. First, Milligan looked to his left at his manager Frank Robinson, who broke into pro ball in 1956. Then, Milligan looked to his right at Leo Gomez, a rookie. Said Milligan: "Nolan has struck out everybody in this room except the trainer."

The only pictures of Nolan Ryan which should be allowed in Cooperstown are those taken after his 40th birthday. Before that age, his career was spectacularly exciting and consistently disappointing. At age 39, his record was 253-226. Then, something happened.

After not having won a strikeout title for seven years, Ryan won the crown at 40, 41, 42 and 43. Twice, he bested Roger Clemens in The Rocket's prime. At 40, Ryan won the ERA title. Finally, at 43 and 44, Ryan got his sixth and seventh no-hitters—giving him as many as the next two men (Sandy Koufax and Bob Feller) combined. How do you strike out 301 men in 239 innings at age 42?

"He gradually learned how to pitch," said Tommy McCraw, who'd watched Ryan's whole career. "I swear…he's getting better. Every year, a little better. He's gone from no control to good control and now he's finally got command of everything."

"Ryan is 150 percent better today than ever in his career," said Frank Robinson in '91. And Robby played with the Express when he set the all-time record with 383 strikeouts in 1973. "The hitter almost has no chance."

William Butler Yeats once surveyed the bright friends of his youth and wrote of them, "Not a finish worthy of the start." What do poets know? Let's remember Ryan as we see him here. Dignified and, finally, in full command of his gift. That's 5,714 strikeouts, thank you very much. If some new kid strikes out 300 men a year for 19 straight seasons, Ryan will still hold the record. Compared to that mark, DiMaggio's streak is in constant jeopardy.

∧

Dwight Gooden, 1986, Wrigley Field

Greg Maddux, 1993, Wrigley Field

JACK MCDOWELL, 1993, CAMDEN YARDS

ROGER CLEMENS, 1993, CAMDEN YARDS

R O B I N S O N

This picture of Brooks Robinson's swing changed baseball's theories of hitting forever.

Well, not this specific picture. But one almost exactly like it which was taken several years earlier by somebody else.

In his playing days, Charlie Lau, the guru of the modern swing, was often in a grouchy mood. Lau was 6 feet tall and 190 pounds. His teammate—Robinson—was 6-1 and 180 with no visible muscles. When Robinson took his smooth swing, the ball often went over the fence. When Lau swung, it looked like he'd hit the ball with the proverbial rolled-up *Sporting News*.

One day, Lau saw a picture of Robinson in the newspaper which was taken about one frame later than this Iooss classic. Brooks's right hand had already come entirely off the bat—as it always did. Robinson had hit a home run.

"What?" roared Lau. "He's not that big. He's not that strong. How can he hit a home run with *only one hand*? It looks like he's *throwing* the bat."

And, so, the Lau Theory, which has dominated batting cage discussions for the past 20 years, was born. Yes, have the sensation that you are throwing the bat at the ball. Don't grip the bat too tightly. Let your top hand come off the bat a split second after contact. Finish your swing with your weight on your front foot. All totally controversial stuff. And all practiced by superstars from George Brett through Mike Schmidt to Frank Thomas.

If the Brooks photo was Lau's "Eureka," then Tommy John helped him get a better overview of hitting. One day, Lau was expounding on how Brooks, Roberto Clemente and Willie Mays had all unintentionally developed this new technique. As Lau talked about pet teaching points—like hitting off a firm front side,

engthening the arc of the swing, finishing with your hands high and finding a triggering mechanism to initiate the swing—John started laughing.

"What's so funny?" Lau recalled saying.

"You're 50 years too late. Bobby Jones already figured out the golf swing," said John, an avid and excellent golfer. "You've just moved the plane of the golf swing upward so you can hit a moving baseball at waist level rather than a stationary golf ball at ground level."

In time, Lau realized John was, basically, right.

If you still like hitting better the old esthetic Ted Williams way—with balanced weight, both hands always on the bat and a slight, graceful uppercut for extra distance, then blame Brooks Robinson and a picture like this one.

⌃

Bo Jackson, 1989, Arlington Stadium

Johnny Callison, 1964, Connie Mack Stadium

MAYS

DiMAGGIO

MANTLE

Before I met them, I was sure I knew Mickey Mantle, Willie Mays and Joe DiMaggio pretty well. Quite a bit has been written and said about these three guys over the years, don't you know. During your first 10 years in the press box, you hear the stuff reconfirmed, or at least repeated. You figure it can't all be wrong. So, I expected Mantle to be a stupid self-infatuated jerk. I figured I'd love Mays—not only the best but also the most joyous player of my childhood. And I assumed DiMaggio was a complex, brooding mystery.

Don't you just love the way life bites you in the ass every time? All three turned out to be the opposite of what I expected. Or, perhaps, all had simply been changed rather radically by age and the transition from hero to human.

If clubhouse word-of-mouth is worth anything, Mantle must have insulted, offended, or at least irritated every civilized person who met him before he reached the age of 30. By the time he was in his 50s, Mantle was a wonderfully appealing mess of a fellow. He was sad, honest, hurt, sardonically funny, clearly disappointed in himself and trying hard to fix what was left of his life. He didn't mention alcoholism; however, when he wrote about his 43-year battle with the bottle several years later, it certainly seemed appropriate.

Mantle retold a chilling story about a dream that recurred to him throughout his retirement. He could see his old buddies, Whitey Ford, Billy Martin, Yogi Berra and Casey Stengel, in some sort of mound conference. They're saying, "Where's Mickey?"

But Mantle himself is trapped *outside* the park, beyond the center-field fence. In the dream he tries to crawl and claw his way under the fence. He always wakes up sweating. But he never makes it under that fence.

On one hand, Mantle is brutally conscious of how much he misses his youth. Perhaps that awareness allows him to leave the past behind—to a degree—and move into a new present. Of all the players I've met who'd automatically be called legends, Mantle is the only one who seems, almost completely, to have forgotten or discarded that former self.

As a result, Mantle seems both surprisingly humble and quite vulnerable. The degree to which men of a certain age are thunderstruck when they meet him in the flesh is a perpetual, perplexing pleasure to him. Sure, it's weird. But Mantle seems consoled by the thought that he makes people feel good just by shaking their hand or acting civil. How circles love to complete themselves.

Mays is the opposite of Mantle. He's frozen. For years, his clothes were decades out of fashion, as though he were attempting a Sonny Bono imitation. He's never going to be Willie Mays again. He has no new person to become. His story's over. That's horribly unfair. He's mad about it. And he's not planning to get over it. If God showed up at Willie's front door, it would be Judgment Day, all right. But Willie might be the one giving God a piece of his mind.

< WILLIE MAYS, 1966, COUNTY STADIUM

<< REGGIE JACKSON, 1969, OAKLAND-ALAMEDA COUNTY STADIUM

Mays dislikes and resents the kind of intrusive, demanding idol worship from the public that Mantle accepts humbly. While Mantle feels like he has a harmless opportunity to give an innocent gift, Mays acts like everybody is trying to steal something from him. Mantle is flattered and slightly embarrassed that he can make money simply by signing his name. Mays finds it incredible that anybody would think he'd give away his autograph for free.

Mays' basic mood—the attitude of his face in repose—is so bleak and jaded that he might pass for a demimonde burnout. He's only truly animated—suddenly the old Buck once more—when he's in the presence of athletes in a locker room setting. Then he's funny, he's sarcastic, he's profane, he's giggling uncontrollably, he's agitating everybody, he's a god among mortals. He's Willie Mays again, but only for a tiny borrowed sliver of time on a few widely scattered occasions. You can see Mays' point. God has a lot to answer for.

DiMaggio is the biggest surprise of all. He's not mysterious. He's not unapproachable. He's not chilly in conversation. His secret is that he has no secret. He's a quiet, handsome, gentlemanly Italian guy with a natural reserve and not much to say on many subjects. He'll come right out and tell you as much. He'd rather listen than talk. He doesn't set much stock in his own opinion. He likes old friends, family and familiar routines. He's proud of his hard work and craftsmanship as a player. But as to all the fuss that's made over him, he has the natural dignity and common sense to know it's unseemly.

If you don't fawn over DiMaggio, he appreciates it. In fact, he gets along quite easily with those who are too young to have seen him play or to know—to the bone—the ridiculous magnitude of his fame long ago. If you treat him like a slightly boring, well-mannered, good-at-heart, Almost-Average Joe, he sometimes seems downright grateful. People don't climb trees to get a peek at him anymore. It's a relief. The older he gets, the easier it is to be just Joe.

∧

MICKEY MANTLE, 1964, POMPANO BEACH

∧

JOE DIMAGGIO, 1980, YANKEE STADIUM

When he was 46, fat and very retired, Hank Aaron entered a home run hitting contest one sleepy summer afternoon in San Diego against Dave Parker, Dave Winfield and Willie Stargell, who were all still in their prime.

Warming up for the contest, Aaron barely got his bat on half-speed pitches. The crowd murmured its collective embarrassment and empathy. Once the contest started, Aaron swung and missed at the first two pitches from a Pirates' batting practice pitcher. Everybody turned their eyes away.

Pride, however, can work strange wonders. And what player ever had more pride than the neat, diligent, analytical, understated Aaron? On the third of six allotted swings in the round, Aaron whacked a homer. The crowd cheered with relief. Then, the next pitch disappeared over the leftfield center also. Finally, as reporters scrambled back into the press box to watch, a third consecutive pitch disappeared over the fence, propelled by that famous sweet slash of the wrists. All this took, perhaps, 30 seconds. Finally, with his sixth swing, Aaron drove a ball 430 feet to the top of the center-field wall.

Suddenly, everybody was *extremely* interested in the proceedings. Why? Because Aaron's old teammate—Warren Spahn, 59—was due to pitch the final round of the homer hitting contest. Because Spahn and Aaron were teammates on the Braves, they'd never faced each other, not even for fun. Yes, the all-time home run king and the winningest pitcher since the arrival of the lively ball. Not since Babe Ruth faced Walter Johnson for charity when both were in their fifties had such legends met.

Spahn lobbed mushballs to Parker, Stargell and Winfield. Aaron hit last, needing just one homer to beat all the current stars. Spahn peered in, grinned and threw. Aaron swung and missed. He smiled back at Spahn. Spahn threw again. Aaron looked at the pitch as though it were covered with radioactive waste. Although he was due five more swings, Aaron gently laid down his bat, turned his back on Spahn and walked away, ending the contest by fiat.

Back in the dugout, Aaron was asked, "Why'd you quit? Hurt yourself swinging?"

"No," said Aaron brusquely. "Spahn was throwing screwballs."

And they say Walter Johnson threw sliders to Ruth.

HANK AARON AND SATCHEL PAIGE, 1969, PALM BEACH

< HANK AARON, 1969, PALM BEACH

P U C K E T T

Here is an impatient, hungry, ebullient man who can't wait to hit. By nature, rather than design, Puckett *always* hits the first pitch if humanly possible. Attack, attack—that's Puck. In the process, he has uncovered a radical new theory of hitting. Someday, bouncy bubbly, round-as-a-barrel Kirby may be famous as the man who discovered the secret of 21st-century batting: Hit the first strike.

For a generation, hitters have been misled by the dictum preached by Ted Williams, that the smart hitter almost always takes the first pitch. This theory sounds sane, but is, in fact, backasswards. Until the 1990s, baseball didn't have statistics on how batters hit in each count. Now we know.

The league hits 70 points higher (and slugs 130 points higher) on 0-0 pitches than on all other counts combined. In other words, the *average* big leaguer hits and slugs like Stan Musial on 0-0 pitches. It isn't just *some* guys who hit better on 0-0. It's almost *everybody*. (Actually, 95 percent.)

Despite these facts, only 20 percent of first-pitch strikes are put into play.

Are these guys dumb or what? Why take the pitch that everybody murders?

So far, only one hitter has seen the light: Kirby. More than 25 percent of his at bats are over after *one pitch*. That makes him the game's No. 1 free swinger—by a lot. Everybody knows it. But nobody can stop him.

From 1986 through 1994, Puckett was baseball's top hitter (.325). On 0-0 pitches, he batted over .380 and slugged better than .560. In other words, he was a *typical* hitter—i.e., vastly better on 0-0 counts than his overall norm. However, Puckett— almost alone—took advantage of this edge. Every season he has about 100 *more* one-pitch at bats than the league average.

Let's not choke on numbers. The facts are irrefutable. Most big leaguers should be putting the first strike into play *twice as often* as they do. Even then, they wouldn't equal Kirby's 25-percent level. If Puckett ever writes a rebuttal to Williams's *My Turn At Bat*, it will be a mighty short book.

< Kirby Puckett, 1993, Camden Yards

^

Tony Gwynn, 1993, Jack Murphy Stadium

Paul Molitor, 1993, Oakland-Alameda County Stadium >

Carlos Baerga, 1993, Cleveland Municipal Stadium >>

As a player, Frank Robinson wanted both sides of the plate. And he'd pay the price—in fastballs at his head—to have it. His left elbow hung over the inside corner, his eyes bored a hole in the pitcher and the battle was on. You couldn't ask for more in a player or a teammate. But many wondered how Frank's style would wear with the years. After all, no matter how he tries, Bob Gibson can't get that aggrieved at-war-with-the-world tone out of his voice.

It took years, and a couple of firings in San Francisco and Cleveland as a manager, but, slowly, Frank Robinson learned to let life have the outside corner. At least occasionally. The chip on his shoulder—once of cord-wood dimensions—shrank to a toothpick. He stopped scouting for enemies and started prospecting for friends. The culmination of Robby's maturation was on display when he managed the 1988 Orioles—the notorious team which began the season 0-21, with the last 14 defeats coming with Robinson as manager.

"I admire these players. I can't ask 'em to play any harder,"
he said, perhaps knowing that while ugly may only be skin-
deep, bad goes right to the bone. What amazed Robinson
most was the public's tolerance—even its sympathy—with the
horrible team. Robinson had never guessed that complete
failure could be permitted. "You would think people would
act worse, that they'd really be down on you. But they haven't
been." When the team returned home—1-23—a sellout crowd
greeted them with ovations and encouragement.

"Nobody likes to be the joke of the league, but we have
to accept it," said the modern, thoroughly-evolved Robby.
However, in his desk drawer was a lapel pin from a fan which
said: "It's Been Lovely But I Have To Scream Now."

⌃

FRANK ROBINSON, 1966, BALTIMORE MEMORIAL STADIUM

BRETT

In dugouts, one accolade ranks higher than all others: "He's a gamer."

Your favorite glove or bat—the one you save for the game itself—is your "gamer." Nobody in recent times has been summarized more often with that one phrase—"he's a gamer"—than George Brett.

One afternoon in 1980, before people noticed he had a chance to bat .400 that season, Brett showed up at Royals Stadium in Kansas City for a fairly typical day's work. It was 96 degrees. On the Royals' Astroturf field, the temperature was perhaps 120 at ankle level. On such days, players tend to arrive late so the heat won't exhaust them before the game ever begins.

Brett arrived 5 1/2 hours before the game. First, he pitched batting practice to the scrubs who arrive early for "extra work." The ambidextrous Brett pitched lefthanded, looking a lot like his brother Ken, the 14-season southpaw. Next, Brett shagged fly balls for an hour. Then, he took dozens of extra grounders at both third and shortstop. Why shortstop? Who knows.

Finally, Brett did all the normal stuff—batting practice, infield practice with the regulars, then infield with the scrubs as a lefty first baseman.

In the game, he had three hits.

This photo is dead, flat perfect. Brett's surroundings are grimy, ancient and indigenous, right down to the paper cup at his feet for spitting tobacco juice. Brett is as authentic as it gets. Once, after he and Graig Nettles had a brawl in Yankee Stadium, Brett said, "Only one thing impressed me about that fight. Thurman Munson was on top of me in the pile. My arms were pinned, so he put both his hands over my face so his teammates couldn't punch me."

Here we have True Brett: smart, reserved, confident, combative and, perhaps, possessed of a few secrets and a number of scars which are none of your business. All that's lacking is a scab that hasn't quite stopped bleeding.

< *GEORGE BRETT, 1993, ANAHEIM STADIUM*

Dick Allen, 1973, Comiskey Park

DICK ALLEN, 1973, CONSHOHOCKEN, PA

THOMAS

GRIFFEY

GONZALEZ

Camden Yards opened 16 months
before the All-Star Game arrived in 1993.
Architects designed the park so home
runs of historic length—the kind hit
by Babe Ruth, Jimmy Foxx and Mickey
Mantle—could reach symbolic landmarks.
The B&O Warehouse beyond the right-
field wall was 475 feet from home plate.
A 490-foot blow to left field could clear
the bullpens, hit a concrete walk and,
with a few lucky bounces, end up in
downtown Baltimore. In straight left,
the second deck was 480 feet distant.
Somebody would reach it someday.
Nobody discussed the third deck in left
field. It was for people, not home runs.

By the time the All-Star Game arrived,
nobody had hit the warehouse or soared
over the bullpen or landed in the second
deck. Had the designers miscalculated?
Was the current generation not quite up
to snuff?

The mother of all home run hitting
contests was held on the day before the
All-Star Game. A new constellation of
sluggers was on display—Frank Thomas,
Ken Griffey, Jr., Juan Gonzalez and
Michael Jordan.

FRANK THOMAS, 1994, COMISKEY PARK >

^
Ken Griffey, Jr., 1994, Comiskey Park

Ken Griffey, Jr., 1993, Oakland-Alameda County Stadium >

Frank Thomas and Ken Griffey, Jr., 1994, Comiskey Park >>

Maybe the new breed wanted to show off for Air. Griffey hit the warehouse on the fly. At the second-floor level. Then, Thomas cleared the bullpens, sending the ball skipping toward the Babe Ruth Museum two blocks away. Lots of people talked about those blows. Until (Long Gone) Gonzalez came up.

Wire service reports the next day—that Gonzalez's blast into the third deck went "at least 475 feet"—were greatly understated. The left-field fence where Gonzalez's ball struck is six stories high. So, tell me, how far does a high line drive travel if it is still digging hard when it reaches a point 454 feet from home plate and is still six stories in the air? How can 500 feet be the right answer? Maybe 550 feet is too far.

In 1956, Mantle hit a ball measured at 565 feet in Griffith Stadium off Chuck Stobbs. Gonzalez's blow—though merely part of a circus show—may have been the longest since then.

When you look at the portrait of Griffey and Thomas—back-to-back—think historically. Ty Cobb and Honus Wagner. Ruth and Lou Gehrig. Ted Williams and Joe DiMaggio. Mantle and Willie Mays. Junior and the Big Hurt.

By contrast, Walter's study of Gonzalez's physique is a kind of wildlife photo. By 25, Gonzalez had won two home run titles, had a bad back and, one winter, weight lifted his way to 28 more pounds than he weighed in this shot. Whether Gonzalez ends up with 600 lifetime home runs or fizzles, remember this: Nobody these days can launch it like Long Gone. He could pin Air with his pinky.

< JUAN GONZALEZ, 1993, ARLINGTON STADIUM

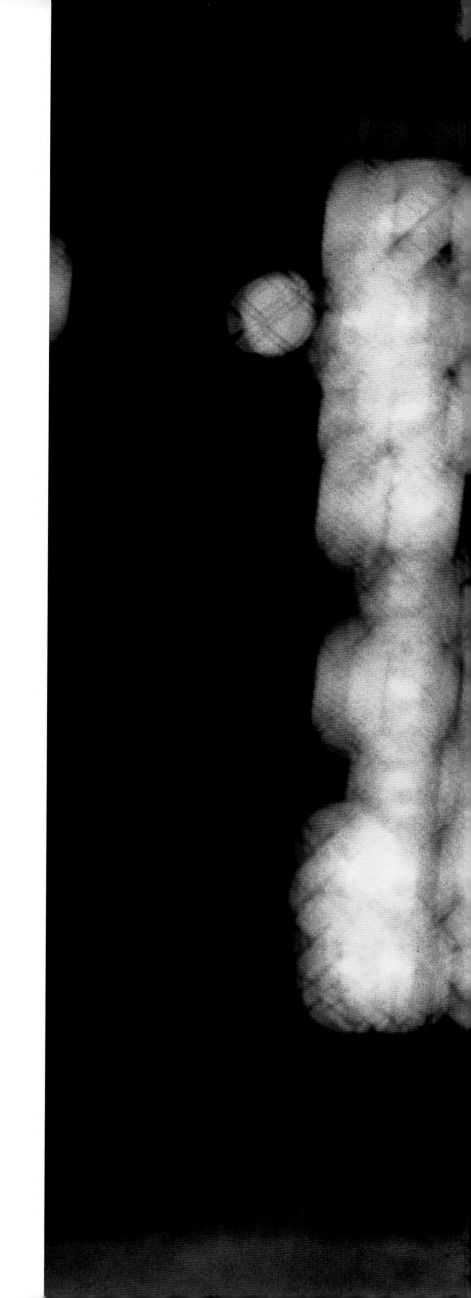

WILLIE RANDOLPH, 1979, METROPOLITAN STADIUM >

Ozzie Smith is the greatest defensive shortstop who ever lived. Lots of people love him. They can have him.

Years ago, I wrote a flattering cover story about Ozzie for *GQ*. When the story came out, Ozzie was criticized by teammates for some controversial quotes. So, Ozzie immediately denied his comments.

My *GQ* editor, who'd also been at the interview where Smith made the comments, laughed when I called him. To help us prepare our story, Smith's agents had sent us a draft of Ozzie's autobiography; *every one* of the statements Smith was denying from coast to coast appeared in the galleys of his own book.

"At least he'll edit that stuff out now," I said.

But he didn't. A couple of months later, Smith's autobiography hit the stands with all those irresponsible, inaccurate *GQ* quotes in his own book.

I'm starting to think Ozzie's never going to apologize.

S A B O

"As a manager, the worst day of your life," Gene Mauch told me, "is when you realize that you care more than the players do."

Once, on an off-day in mid-summer, Chris Sabo and I ended up in the same charity golf tournament. The pennant race that year was terrific. Sabo's Orioles were nip-and-tuck with the Yankees every day. At that point in his career, Sabo was considered a fanatically dedicated throw-back style player.

I told Sabo I'd stayed up past 2 a.m. to hear the end of the Yankees game the previous night in California. New York had won with an incredible ninth-inning rally that put countless Baltimore fans in a sour mood. I expected Sabo to say, "Can you believe those lucky bums?" Or, maybe, he'd ask about some of the inside strategy during the Yankee rally.

Instead, he said, "Yeah? Who won?"

^
CHRIS SABO, 1993, WRIGLEY FIELD

To his intimates, Cal Ripken, Jr., has always been "Calvin," not Cal or Rip or Junior. John Calvin. Calvin Coolidge. Calvin Ripken. A tradition?

The dictionary says that Calvinism "emphasizes the supremacy of the Scriptures in the revelation of truth, the omnipotence of God, the sinfulness of man, the salvation of the elect by God's grace alone and a rigid moral code."

That's so much like Ripken it's spooky. The fundamentals, taught by his father the career coach, constitute the scriptures. The Game is above the flawed men who play it, relentlessly exposing their carelessness or lack of preparation. By patiently and humbly playing the game properly, grace falls upon you like a gift. For the time being, you're one of the elect—though you doubt you entirely deserve it. If you play in more than 2,000 straight games, you do it "one day at a time," because good luck, like grace, is in the game's hands.

Though Ripken is a baseball Calvinist, he's entirely different off the field. He may be the "nicest" modern ballplayer in the traditional American sense of the word.

Once, before an Orioles game, I accidentally slammed the door of my truck on the index finger of an eight-year-old boy.

The injury was minor, but the boy (a friend of my son's) was in lots of pain. My instinctive reaction was to promise him an autographed ball from Cal. That stopped the tears.

Reporters aren't supposed to ask players for autographs. It's an invasion of their locker room privacy, not to mention a blurring of the lines between objective reporter and subject. Still, I sheepishly asked Cal for help.

"I'll leave the ball in my locker," he said.

How long does it take to write, "To Drew. Hope your finger feels better soon. Cal Ripken, Jr." I figured I might be getting blown off.

Later, I found the ball in Ripken's locker—entirely covered with writing. "When I got hurt as a boy," Ripken ended his note, "my dad always told me, 'You'll feel better before you're married twice.' "

That's Ripken. Dutiful, good-hearted, but also a little salty, oblique, bemused and even a tad shaggy dog. He's smarter than you think and also more ironic and detached from his role as Hero. What on earth's that kid going to make of the idea that his finger will stop hurting before he's married twice?

<CAL RIPKEN, 1991, FT. LAUDERDALE

CARL YASTRZEMSKI, 1979, FENWAY PARK >>

Half in shadow, half in light. Wade Boggs, indeed. The bright light is Boggs .335 batting average. The shadow, however, is the great gift he decided never to share with the world—his enormous power-hitting potential. This is a man with about 100 career home runs who, according to those who played with him, could have had 400 easily.

Throughout his career, Boggs put on some of the best tape-measure batting-practice home run hitting displays of his generation. "There's no question that Boggs hit the ball farther and harder than Jim Rice or Dwight Evans or Don Baylor," said old Red Sox pitching coach Bill Fischer who threw batting practice to them for years. "He has titanic power that he hasn't shown....He regularly hits the ball onto the roof in [old] Comiskey Park and into the waterfalls in Kansas City. He'll hit 10 home runs in one round of batting practice....He could hit as many homers as he wanted."

"He outdistances any of us," confirmed Baylor, referring to himself (338 career homers), Rice (382) and Evans (385). "It's not close."

Yet only once in his career has Boggs hit a dozen home runs in a season. His RBI totals are pathetic—one every nine at bats. Just as Gene Mauch manages as though the ball were still dead, Boggs bats as though the calendar says 1911 and he's trying to beat Ty Cobb for the batting title.

Just once, Boggs tried to emerge as a combination hitter-slugger—in 1987, when he had 24 homers, yet won the batting title at .363. Even then, as he tried to go for the fences more, he was ill at ease and talked about how he was not psychologically prepared to give up any significant chunk of his batting average, even for a bushel of home runs. Later, after the Margo Adams scandal, Boggs retreated to the security of sliced singles to left field.

"Nobody can take a batting title away from me," Boggs said.

∧

WADE BOGGS, 1992, FENWAY PARK

< *WADE BOGGS, 1990, FENWAY PARK*

T R A M M E L L

W H I T A K E R

Trammell and Whitaker played side-by-side longer than any keystone combo in major league history. Sometimes, people called them Lou Trammell and Allan Whitaker. Both deserve to be in the Hall of Fame. One or both probably won't make it. The reason? They were so smooth and effortlessly graceful on the field, and so utterly self-effacing off it, that baseball writers— the people who vote for the Hall of Fame—seldom paid any attention to them. They were Detroit's squeakless wheels. I was as guilty as any. I've never spoken to Whitaker and only talked to Trammell once for two minutes—getting quotes for a story on somebody else. Yet I bet I've spent more time yacking with Sparky Anderson than all my cousins combined.

LOU WHITAKER AND ALAN TRAMMELL, 1992, ANAHEIM STADIUM >

ALAN TRAMMELL, 1993, TIGER STADIUM >>

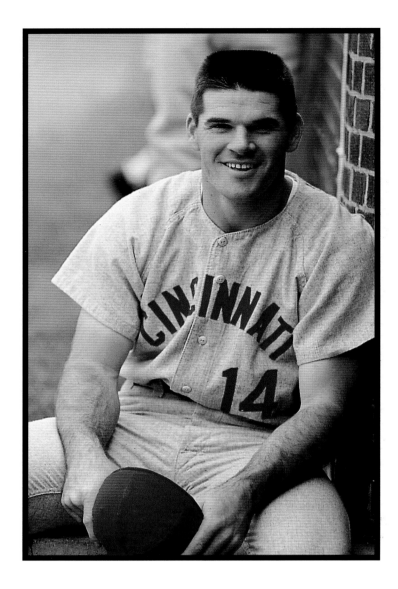

During the 1989 season, after he was banished from baseball, people looked at Pete Rose as if he were a man from Mars. His every word and gesture and personal association was examined and reexamined in light of his banishment for allegedly gambling on games of the Cincinnati team he'd managed.

One night that summer, I sat with Rose in the mezzanine deck of Riverfront Stadium, watching the Reds. Rose hadn't gone to jail yet for tax evasion, but he was surrounded by rumors. We'd known each other for 15 years. He was the friendliest, funniest, most helpful and unpretentious player I'd ever covered. Painfully uneducated and narrow, sure. But a bad guy at heart?

Rose knew I was writing about him and that, like everybody else, I would be alert to any telltale signs of flawed character, or lack of self-knowledge, which might help readers understand how a man could fall so far.

Rose ordered a beer from a waitress. When she gave him the check, Rose, with considerable difficulty and wiggling, managed to screw his hand down into the pocket of his skin-tight polyester slacks and pull out a money clip. In that clip was several thousand dollars, all in $100 bills. "Here, honey," Rose said, peeling one off the top.

Rose gave no thought to the symbolism of that fist-sized roll of C notes—an image right out of a film noir gangster movie. How do we arrive at the places where we end up? And why don't they provide mirrors along the way?

∧
PETE ROSE, 1968, WRIGLEY FIELD

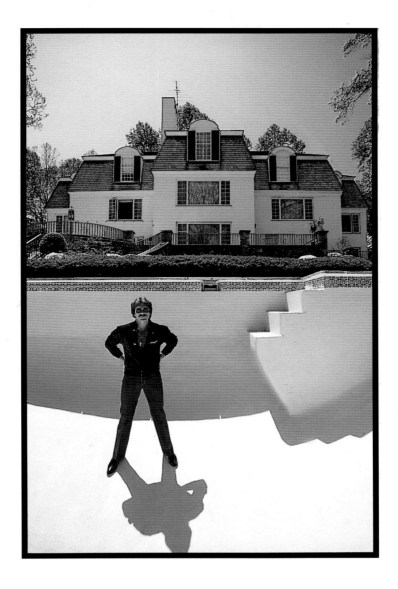

Statistics lie. Mike Schmidt is proof. On paper, he seems to have been almost identically productive through a 14-season period from 1974 through 1987, averaging 37 homers, 104 RBI, 99 runs and 98 walks. However, Schmidt himself believes that his career was altered radically by one pitch in the 1979 All-Star Game.

Before that season, Schmidt was a dangerous hitter, but not a complete one. The toughest pitchers, in the most important situations, with the game on the line, could almost invariably get him out if they made good pitches. Usually, they struck him out. In the key at-bats that mattered most, Schmidt considered himself a mere "mistake hitter," hoping to get lucky. That drove him nuts.

So, in the mid-career when most superstars would never dream of tampering with the source of their success, Schmidt changed much of his approach to hitting. He adopted and modified many of the ideas of the late Charlie Lau. Instead of being a dead pull hitter, Schmidt taught himself to be an "alley hitter," who waited a bit longer before committing himself to swing. He learned to stand off the plate, then stride toward it, a style called "charging the plate." Thus, Schmidt sacrificed a bit of power but gained considerable plate coverage. Most important, he suddenly felt that he was waiting for the ball to come to him, rather than impatiently lunging to get to the ball before it sped past him.

For Schmidt, the litmus test of his new method came when he faced Nolan Ryan in the All-Star Game. "He threw me a perfect curveball on the outside corner," remembered Schmidt. "I waited and I lined a double off the right-center-field wall. That one at-bat changed my whole career. From then on, I considered myself a real hitter, not just a slugger."

⌃

MIKE SCHMIDT, 1975, AT HOME

∧

VIC POWER, 1962, YANKEE STADIUM

<< JOHNNY BENCH, 1974, FULTON COUNTY STADIUM

SMOKY BURGESS AND ELROY FACE, 1963, FORBES FIELD >

What does baseball sound like? It sounds like Earl Weaver.

Once, I was interviewing him in the dugout during the "Star Spangled Banner." Muttering to himself, cigarette cupped in his hand like a schoolboy, Weaver said, "The horseshit cameras are always trying to catch me smokin' during the anthem." After a pause, he said out of the blue, "I smoke these fuckin' Raleighs 'cause with 50,000 coupons they give you a brass coffin."

In this photo—my favorite in the book—Earl is down in the tunnel that runs from the Orioles' dugout to their locker room. Walter, skulking around, has shot him silhouetted against the right-field light stanchion. Maybe Weaver has been ejected for kicking dirt on home plate or ripping third base out of its moorings or pecking an ump in the nose with the bill of his cap; the umps can't see him in the tunnel, but he can manage the game from there anyway. On the other hand, maybe Earl just can't bear to watch Don Stanhouse walk the bases full with a one-run lead in the ninth, so he's down in the dank tunnel, too tortured to watch what he can't control, peeking out between pitches. Or, maybe, he's just enacting one of his countless superstitions: "Every time I fail to smoke a cigarette between innings, the other team will score."

Listening to Weaver talk was often better than the game. He was so smart, funny, mean, blunt, perceptive, crude, vain and volatile that his whole attitude amounted to a kind of little man's cosmic insubordination.

One day, when he saw a slumping Al Bumbry going to chapel before a Sunday afternoon game, Earl snapped, "Take your bat with you." After reluctantly removing Mike Cuellar from the pitching rotation, he said, "I gave him more chances than my first wife." Weaver swore so much that devout Scott McGregor sat at the opposite end of the bench from Weaver all season. "Scotty said he didn't want to be nearby when Earl got hit by lightning," said Jim Palmer.

The Orioles claimed Weaver never had a drink from the time he woke up in the morning until after the game that night. Then, he sometimes didn't stop. Said one Orioles GM, "Earl has killed more brain cells than most managers ever had."

Nobody told stories better: "In the minors, I saw a guy retire while he was going down the first-base line. By the time he got to the bag he had his hat and shirt off and he just kept right on goin'. Never played another game. I also had a guy climb over the center-field fence and never come back."

And nobody enjoyed eccentric, intelligent or independent players more. Without fines, without rules, by sheer force of personality, Weaver proved that you could get modern players to be as studiously committed to the game as any train-riding old-timers in the '30s. "Earl doesn't care if your hair is down to your ass and you wear 10 pounds of beads," said coach Ray Miller, "but you better take pride in your work."

Every summer, frazzled by the race, Weaver would long for the lethe of retirement. "Just once I want to see the sky turn to dusk without the stadium lights coming on."

As much as anything, Weaver loved to argue, debate, throw tantrums—anything to stir everybody up so he could see what made them tick. Three times over the years, Weaver swore he'd never speak to me again. Once, he kept his word for six months. Then, at spring training, he marched up and said, "My wife tells me I'll go to hell if I don't start talking to you again."

"Thanks, Earl," I answered, "but I don't have any questions today." Who says you can't learn from the master?

∧

CASEY STENGEL, 1964, ST. PETERSBURG

< *EARL WEAVER, 1979, MEMORIAL STADIUM*

GENE MAUCH, 1964, CONNIE MACK STADIUM >>

The strike that killed the 1994 World Series probably produced only one hero of conscience: simple, decent, syntax-mangling Sparky Anderson. He risked being blackballed by refusing to manage a scab team. While others injured the game for the sake of self-interest, Sparky—60 years old and none too secure in his Tiger job—jeopardized his future because…well…he could do no other. As Casey Stengel or Martin Luther might've said, "Who'd have thunk it?"

Over the years, Sparky gabbed so much you never suspected he actually meant much of it. Nobody ever saw Sparky change his mind on any subject—unless somebody new came into the room. Anderson once endorsed three different men for American League Manager of the Year—each in his own hometown.

Yet he had a core. "Sparky Anderson?" he'd say. "I'm George Anderson."

From the day the owners canceled the 1994 Series, they waited—like spoiled rich kids on Christmas morning—for the next spring training. Which superstars would betray their union to play alongside the truck drivers who'd populate the owners' replacement teams?

To the owners' shamed amazement, the first future Hall of Famer to cross the imaginary picket line went the wrong way! Sparky didn't come in. He went out. "I will not compromise my beliefs for any amount of money," said Anderson, about to earn $1 million for the first time in 42 years in baseball. "If I did that, I could not live with myself. I will not bargain my integrity."

Sparky'd managed Johnny Bench, Joe Morgan, Pete Rose, Tony Perez, Tom Seaver, Jack Morris, Kirk Gibson, Cecil Fielder, Lou Whitaker and Alan Trammell. He wasn't going to lead a bunch of slapstick bums into Tiger Stadium—the park Ty Cobb, Charlie Gehringer and Hank Greenberg called home. They ordered Sparky to manage a bunch of donkeys who should have been hired to drag the infield, not play on it. And he just wouldn't do it. His sorrow-filled mug became the very symbol of the torture inflicted on his sport.

^

SPARKY ANDERSON, 1975, TAMPA BAY

SPARKY ANDERSON, 1993, TIGER STADIUM >

RICE

Jim Rice was a superior hitter, a hard worker and a decent citizen. In a baseball generation with far too many drug addicts, compulsive gamblers, wife beaters and all-purpose sociopaths, Rice never did anything wrong. Yet, in the big leagues, he received little sympathy when injuries and poor eyesight ended his career early. When he retired, the Red Sox did not even give him a "Day" in thanks for his 1,451 RBI.

Why?

Because, day in and day out, Rice may have been the most unpleasant man in baseball. Except for longtime friends, Rice was intimidating or rude to almost everybody. If somebody'd made a "Go to Hell" sign, he'd have worn it. Once, told about the trade of a teammate, Rice had no idea who the player was.

Only one ballplayer ever threatened me. Rice said he'd stuff me in a trash can if I kept asking him about an incident when he knocked down an umpire at home plate. Naturally, I asked him which trash can he'd like me to get into so I could save him the trouble. Once, at an All-Star Game, Rice started jawing at me about something. To my amazement, three players told him to shut up.

Manners don't count much in the bigs. Rice was the exception that proved the rule.

JIM RICE, 1981, WINTER HAVEN

P A R K E R

When society overpraises and overpays people in one corner of its culture, some of them are naturally going to overvalue themselves. Dave Parker won back-to-back batting titles as the free agent era arrived in the late '70s. He never recovered from his good fortune. If the '80s was the "Me Decade," then Parker devolved into the "Me Ballplayer."

Inundated with wealth and praise, Parker turned from a hard-nosed star on the world champion '79 Pirates into a hard-ass bad actor in the '80s. In this picture, we see Parker at a crossroads: young, lean and trying to decide which way to go. Become an adult like Willie Stargell, whom he loved? Or let the angry adolescent bully have free reign for a few years?

Give a man a few million dollars and, often, he'll show what's in him, all the way down to the bottom of the pot. Once, the Cobra got so fat that he looked more like the Anaconda—one which'd swallowed a sheep. He was a star witness, not a coveted role, at the infamous Pittsburgh Cocaine Trial.

Asked why he wore the Star of David around his neck, Parker said, "Because my name is David and I'm a star." As he aged, Parker wised up and reprised the Stargell role as Pops. Or was that just one last con job?

∧

DAVE PARKER AND GRANT JACKSON, 1980, BRADENTON

F I S K

Whatever was most difficult always fascinated Carlton Fisk the most. The hardest position was the one he wanted. So, it's fitting that the major league record for most games played as catcher is 2,226 by Fisk. For two dozen years, Pudge was a human bruise. He loved it. He hated it. He groused about it. He gloried in it. He called catching "the Dorian Gray position" because "on the outside you look young, but on the inside, you're aging fast. You're afraid one day you'll take off the equipment and discover you've turned to dust." After saying that, he played another 15 seasons.

Fisk wasn't to every taste. That block-letter sign above his locker—"THINK"—implied that, perhaps, others in the same locker room might not be concentrating hard enough. And that enormous dolly full of weight-lifting equipment which he dragged all over America for a decade so he could work out *after games* for 90 minutes certainly showed up the lazy work habits of others.

One anecdote will always capture Fisk's starchy, rigorous New Hampshireman's pride in craftsmanship. One night Deion Sanders—then a rookie—did not run out a pop-up. Even though

Sanders was on the other team, Fisk was so furious that he ran after Sanders, cursing him like a harpooner and threatening to fight on the spot if Neon Deion didn't run. Sanders ran, all right, if only to get away from the 240-pound moralist. Next time, Sanders muttered something about "plantation days" being over. Fisk stopped the game and gave Sanders another lecture, right at home plate, on how Hank Aaron and Willie Mays weren't too fancy to run out their pop-ups and how there was only one right way to play baseball—"the big league way." Sanders later said he appreciated Fisk's view.

Fisk's face in repose doesn't look contemporary. It's not "happy." Nor is it primarily concerned with such an easy pursuit. Instead, it is proud and private. Here, indeed, is a dinosaur we'll sorely miss. For 24 years, you could watch Carlton Fisk at Fenway Park or Comiskey Park. Now, he might as well be in Jurassic Park. Hopefully, Cooperstown will ask for one of Fisk's broken finger-nails, snapped by a foul tip, in case anybody ever wants to clone the ultimate smart, stubborn, tough, clutch-hitting catcher. Of course, the next century might not know what to do with a Carlton Fisk if it had one.

< *CARLTON FISK, 1973, FENWAY PARK*

SCOTT

A huge, exotic necklace, worthy of a harpooner on a South Seas whaler, often hung around the neck of George (Boomer) Scott. He'd hold it up, grin wolfishly and say, "Second basemen's teeth."

< *GEORGE SCOTT, JIM PERRY AND EARL BATTEY, 1967, FENWAY PARK*

∧
GOOSE GOSSAGE, 1980, YANKEE STADIUM

REGGIE JACKSON, 1980, YANKEE STADIUM >

M ATTINGLY

Celebrity, our contemporary aphrodisiac of choice, is customarily viewed as a combination kiss and curse. At a certain level of notoriety, we assume that it becomes impossible for a person to act normally or be treated as though he were not, above all else, famous.

Thank heaven for Don Mattingly. He's proved it's possible to be Most Valuable Player, and a superstar Yankee of the George Steinbrenner era, without becoming an egomaniac. The son of a postman, Mattingly has not mystique, aura or charisma. Everything Reggie Jackson wanted to be, Mattingly wouldn't take if you gave it to him free. Mattingly loved baseball—just baseball. All the rest just made him curl up the corner of his mouth in bemusement.

Most people can tell, instinctively, how others want to be treated. How do we do it? Body language? Intuition? Mattingly wanted to be treated like a normal person. And people sensed it. They let him blend into the woodwork. A modest man is a modest man. And the world, for the most part, knows how to respect it.

For example, Mattingly frequently took infield practice *at shortstop*. Hardly anybody noticed. Okay, maybe the reason was because Mattingly switched from his southpaw's first baseman's mitt and played shortstop *right-handed*.

"It's his fantasy to play shortstop righthanded [in the majors]," Yankee Roy White once told me. "It's amazing. He looks like a pretty good shortstop."

^

Don Mattingly, 1992, Ft. Lauderdale

< Roger Maris, 1962, Yankee Stadium

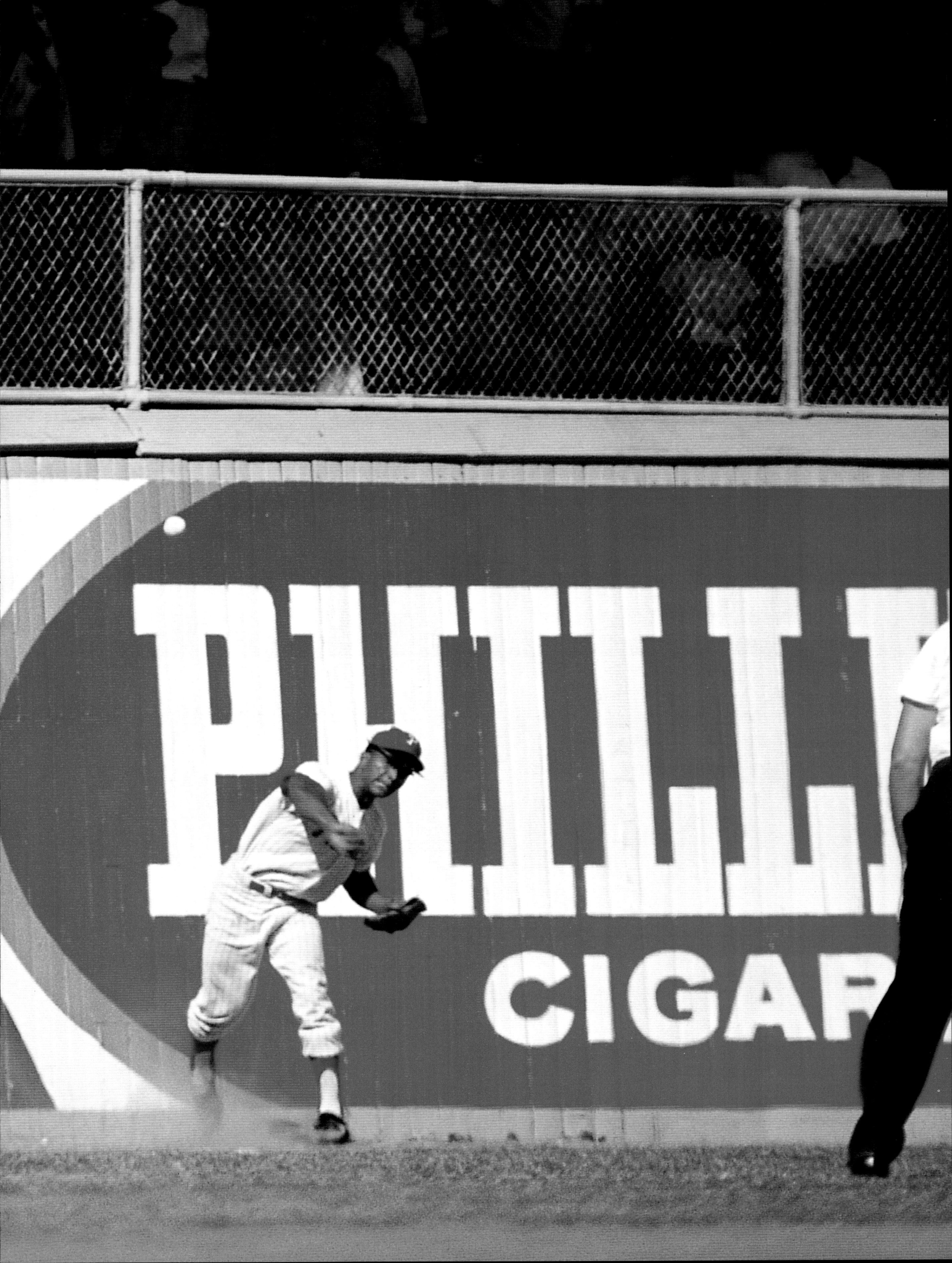
PHILL
CIGAR

^
JULIAN JAVIER AND MIKE RYAN, 1967, FENWAY PARK

<< TONY GONZALEZ, 1966, CONNIE MACK STADIUM

Brooks Robinson, 1968, Memorial Stadium

Y O U N T

You probably think that Robin Yount is the most boring, invisible superstar ever to get 3,000 hits. That's what he wants you to think. He doesn't want you to know that he's a daredevil, a speed freak, a risk taker. It's his business.

However, some know the truth. On the eve of Yount's 3,000th hit, ESPN begged Yount's lifelong friend Rick Dempsey to let them have a copy of the most famous home movie in baseball. (Okay, not including Wade and Margo.)

"Robin said, 'Nope. Let's keep our private lives to ourselves,'" laments Dempsey.

Oh, let's not.

Look at Yount's face. It's got Pony Express rider or first mate on the *Pequod* or NASCAR driver written all over it. This guy isn't going to die in bed. Right now, he's out there, somewhere, doing something you'd never dare. Let it be added that Yount's lifelong friend, Dempsey, is a unique exhibit himself. Rick's wife says if she wakes up in the night and hears a swishing sound over her head, she knows not to sit up. It's Rick practicing his swing in the dark.

Every year at family reunions, the Yount family shows the home movie that Dempsey filmed of Yount years ago when Yount was at the peak of his career. Naturally, when Dempsey got a new video camera for a toy, he suggested that Yount take his motorcycle into a mountain canyon so they could film some stunts. Yount would ride around the circular edge of this crater, going faster and faster, until on the fifth loop, he'd swoop down and head full-bore at the camera like he was going to wipe Dempsey out. Of course, Yount would pop a wheelie and stop right in front of the lens.

Sounds like a great idea, right? But you have to be careful with the Demper's high concepts. Rick once said he thought it was wrong to move the left-field fence in Yankee Stadium—out near the monuments to Babe Ruth and others in Death Valley. "They shouldn't move those graves," said Dempsey.

The movie was going grand until the front wheel of Yount's motorcycle imbedded itself in a mudhole at the bottom of the canyon. "The bike flips and fires [Robin] over the front handlebars right at me. I don't know how far he flew. A long way, head first. He lands, helmet buried in the mud, at my feet.

"I said, 'I'm with Robin Yount here today, doing his famous motorcycle stunts. It's a good thing Bud Selig (Brewers' owner) isn't here with us.

"'So, Robin, how many vertebrae did you just crush? Are you alive?'"

Yount muttered, "I think I'm okay."

< ROBIN YOUNT, 1992, COUNTY STADIUM

K O U F A X

Even in black silhouette, without any conventional clue to his identity, Sandy Koufax is so recognizable that you practically gasp when you first see this photograph; instantly, you know you're gazing at the greatest pitcher of all time at the split second when his bow is most fully taut. This moment, and the next, are the ones the rest of us will never know.

In 1966, at the age of 30, after going 27-9 with a 1.73 ERA and 317 strikeouts, Koufax retired—making my 18-year-old heart feel as sad as a small child's. He was gone and I had never gotten to see him pitch in person.

"I didn't believe it when I heard it," said Don Sutton. "I called Sandy that day. He said, 'There are some things in life I might be jeopardizing if I keep pitching with this elbow…you know, I might want to swing a golf club sometime during the rest of my life.'"

For the next five years, Koufax did some TV work. Then, he disappeared from the game's radar screen for eight years. "I wasn't looking for anything…just looking for time. It was a mindless period to do what I wanted to do and go where I wanted to go. I decided to take a few years for myself. I wanted to see how long I could stretch it."

In 1979, Koufax returned as a Dodger pitching coach. "I need the money," he said. "I'm like a lot of older people living on fixed incomes. I need a regular supplemental income just to keep up with inflation.

"Sooner or later, you say, 'That's enough of that.' You need to find something to do, another purpose. Also, it's hard to be away from possibly the only thing you ever did really well."

Two years later, before a World Series game in Chavez Ravine, I was walking behind the batting cage. A gap appeared between the reporters and players leaning against the cage. There, framed on the mound, almost as you see him here, but now aged 45, was Sandy Koufax—pitching batting practice.

Steve Garvey, Dusty Baker and Ron Cey were taking turns in the cage. As they swung and missed, Koufax's pitches smashed into the tarp at the back of the cage, inches from my feet.

Pitching off the rubber, Koufax threw nothing but fastballs. Garvey swung five times. Baker swung three times. Cey, too. Nobody got the ball out of the cage. Glances were being exchanged around the cage. Next round: Garvey four swings, Baker five, Cey four. Still, nothing but misses and fouls. Next time up, Garvey made the universal flip-of-the-wrist signal for a curve-ball. It must've dropped two feet. Garvey couldn't even swing.

Suddenly a Dodger coach raced to the mound and whispered in Koufax's ear. Immediately, Koufax seemed to come out of a trance, nodding, "Yes, yes." Quickly, he walked off the mound and the other coach pitched the rest of BP.

A World Series game was to begin in 45 minutes and Sandy Koufax, retired for 15 years, was on the verge of destroying the confidence of the heart of the Dodger batting order. Somebody had to get him off that mound, quick, before he could throw a dozen more synapse-tangling curves.

However, they weren't fast enough. A couple of dozen of us had seen him.

^

Sandy Koufax, 1964, Connie Mack Stadium

Sandy Koufax, 1964, Connie Mack Stadium >

IN SEPTEMBER AND OCTOBER, baseball changes into an almost entirely different sport. Instead of being a game of percentages and techniques, persistence and team chemistry, it becomes a stage for stars. ⚾ Until the pennant race, the playoffs and the World Series arrive after Labor Day, baseball is more a medium for general managers and managers than for messiahs. The GM builds a 25-man talent pool and a farm system, which can survive injury and exhaustion. The manager assumes that, over the long season, his niceties of judgement about personnel and strategy will carry the day. Each player, even the most humble, has many chances to contribute significantly. ⚾ Then, autumn arrives and

FALL

all our quasi-intellectual symposia about Baseball As Metaphor go straight to hell. Maybe, from March to August, baseball is a lot like the lives which most of us lead. Craftsmanship can neutralize talent. Persistence and a semblance of mental health can suffice in the absence of inspiration. The individual depends on the group more than the other way 'round. ⚾ However, when the Big Games arrive in the fall, baseball is just like every other sport. Talent and stage presence count for everything. If you have both these blessings, then your name is Reggie Jackson or Bob Gibson, Sandy Koufax or Lou Brock, Willie Stargell or Orel Hershiser, Frank Robinson or Kirk Gibson, Ron Guidry or Tom Seaver, Johnny Bench or Paul Molitor. If you just have the latter, then you're a one-week legend like Bucky Dent or Mark Lemke

∧

Veterans Stadium, 1980 World Series

JIM LONBORG, 1967 WORLD SERIES, FENWAY PARK

Bernie Carbo or Mickey Hatcher. ⚾ Those who most resent the nature of autumn baseball are the great managers who suddenly find their importance diminished, like Gene Mauch, Tony LaRussa and Earl Weaver. It's not their game anymore and, control freaks that they are, it spooks them. ⚾ There are horses for courses and, in baseball, men for seasons. When there's a chill in the air and the whole season hinges on one fragile luck-logged game, no pro would be so infantile as to think that "the best team" is necessarily going to win. That's when you look down your bench, hoping to see somebody named "Pops" or "Buck" or "Lefty" or "Eck." Somebody who doesn't need to give his last name to get a table at Spago.

W I L L I A M S

C A R T E R

The faces of Joe Carter and Mitch Williams will always be joined. Or, rather, they will always be exactly 60 feet, 6 inches from each other on an October night in Toronto in 1993. In this century, only Bobby Thompson and Ralph Branca have a home run linkage of significantly greater impact and durability.

Over the years, Thompson and Branca became close friends. By the 40th anniversary of the "Shot Heard Around The World," they toured the country together like brothers. Both were successful men, apparently at peace with their opposite ends of the ultimate split second in the ancient Giant-Dodger feud.

Don't expect Carter and Williams to end up in adjacent rockers on the front porch of the same old folks' home some day. When Carter won the World Series with his ninth-inning, come-from-behind, three-run homer in Game Six, it was widely viewed inside the sport as pure poetic justice.

Few, if any, players are more widely viewed as classy, clutch, tough, underrated, and gentlemanly than Carter. He's considered the absolutely ideal teammate and friend. Despite eight 100-RBI seasons, he was barely known before that swing. Conversely, few players are more disliked than Williams, perhaps the most cavalierly irresponsible pitcher of his generation. Williams loved to terrorize hitters with his "Wild Thing" rep and didn't care who he hurt. Once, Earl Weaver benched all his stars in mid-game after Williams hit four Orioles.

"The game will catch up with that bleep someday," Weaver said.

The game did.

MITCH WILLIAMS, 1993, WRIGLEY FIELD

JOE CARTER, 1993, OAKLAND-ALAMEDA COUNTY STADIUM >

LOU BROCK, 1967, FENWAY PARK, WORLD SERIES >>

M c L a i n

I felt I knew Denny McLain even before I got his hand-written hate letter from prison.

"You have to talk about two people—Denny on the mound and Denny off it," Dick Bosman once told me. "I couldn't help but like him, he was such a riverboat gambler. He was born to go out on that mound and set up hitters to make fools of themselves....A guy would hit one eighteen miles foul into the upper deck and McLain would start...cussing him, and he'd strike him out on the same pitch.

"You should have seen him and [manager Ted] Williams....If one guy said it was light, the other would call him a liar and say you couldn't see the hand in front of your face....One day, Denny was getting killed....The outfielders had to get oxygen between innings. Well, Ted yanks him and McLain starts yelling about 'What is all this six-inning shit?'

"McLain goes down the tunnel cussing and Ted's right after him. The whole bench followed 'em down the runway just to watch. They stood toe to toe and screamed for five minutes."

The last .400-hitter, maybe ever. And the last 30-game winner, maybe ever.

"After that," said Bosman, "Ted left him out there to dry up and flake away a few times."

Thereafter, McLain became the founder of The Underminers, a fraternity complete with initiation ceremonies that was, half-seriously, dedicated to undermining Williams' authority.

So, with this as background, it was with great pleasure that I received McLain's plump letter. At first, because of the pulpy, white-lined paper and the big, lazy, junior-high-school scrawl, I thought it was just a standard hate letter from a kid. Then, I saw the prison seal stamped on the envelope along with McLain's inmate number. It was the real McLain, all right. Everybody knew he was in jail. Extortion, I think.

The image of Teddy Ballgame and Denny Hardtime screaming at each other in the tunnel crossed my mind. Some of The Underminers might still be at large in the major leagues. So, I decided not to write back to McLain.

However, I'll never forgive myself for throwing that letter in the trash.

DENNY McLAIN, 1968, TIGER STADIUM

R I V E R S

In a sense, the true heir to Yogi Berra on the Yankees was Mickey Rivers. He was possessed Yoginess. Every anecdote, true or false, attached itself to him. Just as Whitey Ford was in charge of Berraisms, so sardonic Graig Nettles became the wiseguy keeper of the Rivers Legend. Herewith, a brief sampling.

When Rivers heard that Reggie Jackson claimed to have an IQ of 160, Mickey supposedly said, "Out of what? A thousand?"

Mickey and Lou Piniella always went to the racetrack together. Emphasis on *always*. Why was this odd couple so inseparable? "They handicap together," Nettles told me. "Lou studies the Racing Form and Mickey talks to the horses."

When Rivers was eventually traded to the Rangers, Nettles was the first teammate with an explanation for the deal. "They traded him to the only team that's in a state where there's no pari-mutuel wagering," he said. "He can't drive to Louisiana and back before a night game."

JOE MORGAN AND MICKEY RIVERS,
1976 WORLD SERIES, RIVERFRONT STADIUM >

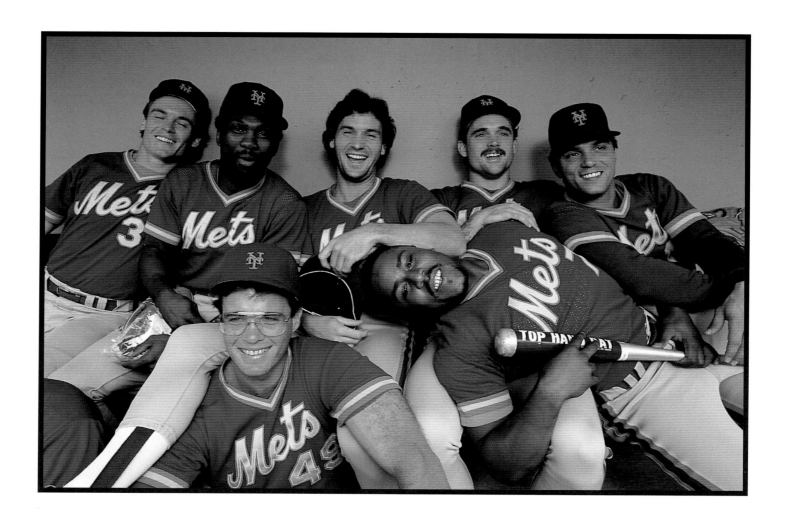

MITCHELL

Here, in one picture is proof of the old locker room adage that "winning is the best deodorant." The adorable, beaming player lying sideways across the laps of his teammates on the bound-for-glory '86 Mets is none other than Kevin Mitchell, one of the most confrontational troublemakers of his generation. Even so, Mitchell couldn't quite match the charm of Mets reliever Randy Myers who, when young, bragged he knew 101 ways to kill a man with his bare hands.

∧

New York Mets, 1986, Dodger Stadium

Darryl Strawberry, 1988, Wrigley Field >

Tony Oliva, 1965, Metropolitan Stadium >>

Here, with his shirt buttons open so his muscles can breathe, and spats on his spikes, with wrist bands and necklaces, with everything but a neon sign that says, "Look at me," we witness the last baseball superstar who also wanted to be a charismatic life-on-display hero: Reggie Jackson.

Since he retired, no one has replaced him. No one wants the job. Too tough.

To be sure, we've seen new players just as good as Buck Tatter Man and some, like Frank Thomas, Ken Griffey, Jr., and Barry Bonds, who are playing at a higher level in the '90s than Reggie ever did in his best seasons.

In the adjacent picture, we see the man who should have been the heir to Jackson—Jose Canseco, the slugger who needs super-catastrophe insurance. His T-shirt says it all about his generation of reluctant heroes: "Leave Me Alone." One year, the A's even hired Reggie to be Jose's personal coach. The job: Give the kid a post-graduate course in "How To Be A Star." Final grade: Incomplete.

Most great pop-culture artists—actors, musicians, athletes—have to love not only their particular gift but also the stage. They realize that their loss of privacy, and the whole unbridled ridiculousness of modern celebrity, must become water off a duck's back if they hope to make the public happy while remaining sane themselves.

In baseball, Reggie was the last of a breed—epitomized by Babe Ruth, Dizzy Dean and Pete Rose—who wanted to lead mythological lives. Reggie called himself "The Straw That Stirs the Drink" and talked about "The Magnitude of Being Me." He fought with Billy Martin and George Steinbrenner on the back pages of the New York tabloids and named a candy bar after himself.

Yet, by the end, even Reggie was frazzled. "I wouldn't be Reggie Jackson for all the money in the world....His entire life is public," said his late-career manager Gene Mauch.

"I'd be me for all the money in the world," laughed Jackson when he was 40. "But it's tough...the average person has absolutely no idea what I go through. It gets easier as you get older...but it bothered me a long time. At one time or another, I've come across as everything—a good guy, a bastard, humble, an egomaniac. I got called an egomaniac a lot more than I liked. I know I'm fallible, flawed, but I think I'm a nice man. What I've been, through it all, is human."

Since Jackson, only one athlete in any sport has endured a comparable level of total-scrutiny inspection: Michael Jordan. As you may have noticed, Air had to retire for almost two seasons simply to reassemble the pieces of his head after the murder of his father and speculation that he was a compulsive gambler.

When he returned, the omnipresent Jordan—"Ad Man to the Universe" and "Economic Lynchpin of the Entire NBA"—summed up the dilemma: "The game is my refuge. On the court, I'm in my dream world and nobody can bother me."

^

Jose Canseco, 1990, Oakland

< *Reggie Jackson, 1980, Yankee Stadium*

Yaz's career stats are pretty phony. In 23 seasons, he hit more than 23 homers only four times. He was a very good player who had a couple of mythical years, then batted .300 only *once* in his last 13 years. But he lasted forever, indefatigably piled up the big numbers and, in the end, was loved by everyone.

And that's how it should have been. Nobody ever wanted to play baseball more than Yaz. Once, during batting practice in the 1978 pennant race, his wrist hurt so badly that he yelled in pain and dropped the bat after every swing. Yaz immediately demanded that the trainer tape the bat to his hand for the rest of the day so that he could still be the designated hitter.

That seemed like a brilliant idea. For about 10 seconds. Until they asked Yaz how he was going to slide into second base with a bat tied to his hand.

"Oh, shit," said Yaz.

But he'd have done it if they'd let him.

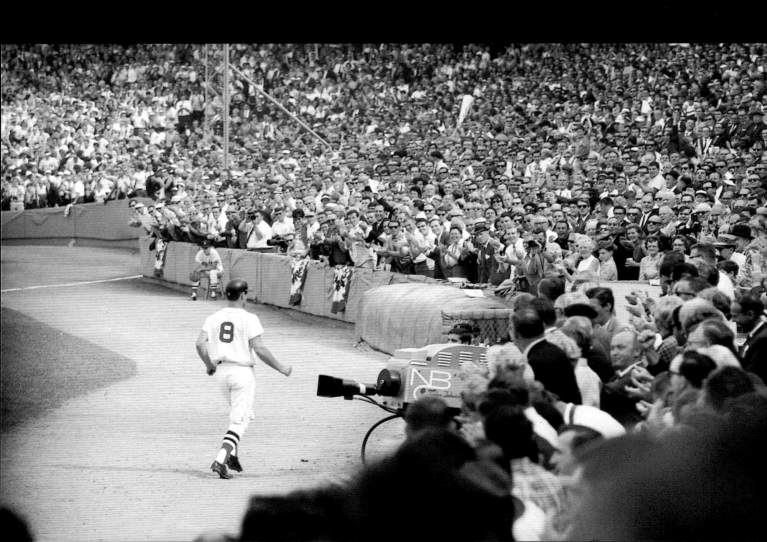

∧

Carl Yastrzemski, 1967, Fenway Park

< Carl Yastrzemski, 1967, Fenway Park

<< Dallas Green, 1980, League Championship Series, Veterans Stadium

SANDY KOUFAX AND DON DRYSDALE, 1965 WORLD SERIES, METROPOLITAN STADIUM